ANIMALS ARE AMAZING

# GORILLAS

BY KATE RIGGS

W
FRANKLIN WATTS
LONDON • SYDNEY

First published in the UK in 2013 by
Franklin Watts
338 Euston Road
London NW1 3BH

Franklin Watts Australia
Level 17/207 Kent Street
Sydney NSW 2000

First published by Creative Education,
an imprint of the Creative Company
Copyright © 2012 Creative Education
International copyright reserved in all countries.
No part of this book may be reproduced in any
form without written permission from the publisher.

ISBN 978 1 4451 1923 6
Dewey number: 599.8'84

A CIP catalogue record for this book is
available from the British Library.

Printed in China

Franklin Watts is a division of Hachette Children's
Books, an Hachette UK company
www.hachette.co.uk

Design and production by The Design Lab
Art direction by Rita Marshall

Photographs by Dreamstime (Eric Gevaert), Getty
Images (Ian Nichols, Kate Roberts), iStockphoto
(Guenter Guni, Phil Hess, Eric Isselée, Marcel Mooij,
Sharon Morris, William Murphy, Ricky Russ, Dave
Thomasnz)

# CONTENTS

# What are gorillas?

*Like all apes, gorillas have eyes that face forwards.*

A gorilla is a type of ape. Apes are animals called **primates**. Gorillas are the largest primate in the world. There are four different kinds of gorilla.

**primates**  humans, apes and monkeys are all primates. Primates have eyes that face forwards and hands that can grip well.

# Big gorillas

Gorillas have a big body and a large head. They have long arms and shorter back legs. Male gorillas can grow to be 1.8 metres tall – as tall as an adult person! Gorillas normally move around on all four **limbs** but they can also stand up on their back legs. Gorillas have black or brownish hair covering their bodies.

*Gorillas can climb trees, but they prefer to move around on the forest floor.*

**limb** a limb is an arm or a leg. Gorillas (and people) have two arms and two legs.

# Strong gorillas

Male gorillas sometimes stand up on their back legs and beat their chests with their hands. This shows other gorillas how big and strong they are! A gorilla's arms are very powerful. They are much stronger than an adult human's. But gorillas are also very gentle animals, they only use their strength if they need to.

*Around the age of 12, the hair on a male gorilla's back turns grey. They are called a 'silverback' when this happens.*

# Where gorillas live

*Gorillas live in forests because they eat the plants that grow there.*

All wild gorillas live in forests in countries located in central and western Africa. Some gorillas like to live in **mountain** forests. Others like to live lower down in **swampy** forests.

**mountain** a very tall hill made of rock.
**swamp** areas of land that are covered with water and trees.

# Gorilla food

Gorillas eat plants. Bamboo, wild celery and thistles are some of their favourite plants. They will also eat some flowers, fruits and bark from trees. Gorillas have sharp teeth that can tear through tough plants. Sometimes they also eat ants or other insects. Gorillas don't need to drink much water. The plants they eat contain most of the water they need to survive.

*This gorilla is eating wild celery, one of its favourite foods.*

# New gorillas

A mother gorilla has one baby at a time. Babies grow quickly. They drink their mother's milk and eat leaves and fruits. They can cling to their mother's hair. This helps them to stay safe from **predators**. Baby gorillas like to wrestle and play. They swing from tree branches and make a lot of noise! Gorillas can live for more than 35 years in the wild.

*Baby gorillas love to play together.*

**predators** animals that kill and eat other animals.

# Life in a troop

Gorillas live in family groups called troops. There can be up to 30 gorillas in a troop. They all eat together and will **groom** each other's hair. A **dominant** silverback leads the troop. He helps them find food and protects the troop from predators such as leopards.

*Members of a gorilla troop take care of each other.*

**groom** to get rid of dirt and insects.
**dominant** in the animal world this means the strongest member of the group. He will often be the oldest and the biggest, too.

# Sleepy gorillas

Gorillas spend most of their time eating and sleeping. Adult gorillas eat up to 27 kilogrammes of food a day! Gorillas take a lot of naps during the day. At night, they sleep for 13 to 15 hours. They build a nest from branches and leaves to sleep in.

*Baby gorillas share their mother's nest when they go to sleep.*

# Gorillas and people

**People** love gorillas because they are so like us. No two gorillas have the same **fingerprints** – just like people. And gorillas can 'talk' to each other with sounds like grunts, barks and howls. People go to Africa to see gorillas in the wild. It is fun to see these large apes up close! Gorillas are **endangered** and national parks help to protect the wild gorillas that live in them.

*These two gorillas are 'talking' to each other.*

**fingerprints** the patterns in the skin on the ends of your fingers.
**endangered** an animal or plant that only has a small number of them left on Earth.

# A Gorilla Story

**Why** do gorillas do nothing but eat and sleep all day long? People who live near the Congo River in Africa tell a story about this. Long ago, it rained so much that the river flooded. The gorillas helped all the animals to get to dry ground – even the fish! But fish need water to live. All the other animals made fun of the gorillas for their mistake. From then on, the gorillas stopped doing anything except eating and sleeping.

# Useful information

## Read More

*Saving Wildlife: Mountian Animals* by Sonya Newland
(Franklin Watts, 2010)

*Protecting Our Planet: Habitats and Wildlife in Danger* by Sarah Levete
(Wayland, 2009)

## Websites

*http:// kids.nationalgeographic.co.uk/kids/animals/creaturefeature/
mountain-gorilla/*
This site has lots of facts, photos and a video of the mountain gorilla.

*http://gowild.wwf.org.uk/africa*
This WWF site has a section on Africa including a fact file on the
gorilla, a picture puzzle and a story.

*http://www.koko.org/kidsclub/*
Learn about a famous gorilla named Koko and her friends.

Every effort has been made by the Publishers to ensure that these websites are suitable
for children, that they are of the highest educational value and that they contain no
inappropriate or offensive material. However, because of the nature of the Internet, it is
impossible to guarantee that the contents of these sites will not be altered. We strongly
advise that Internet access is supervised by a responsible adult.

## Index